TECHNIQUE AND DESIGN OF CLUNY LACE

Young lacemaker earlier this century.

Technique and design of

Cluny Lace

by L. Paulis
translated and enlarged by
M. Rutgers

RUTH BEAN
Carlton, Bedford, 1984

Published by Ruth Bean, Victoria Farmhouse, Carlton,
Bedford MK43 7LP, England.
Translated and enlarged from the French language original:
*La Dentelle aux Fuseaux, Première Partie: Dentelles à fil continu.
I: Cluny,* by L. Paulis, Brussels, Maurice Lamertin 1921.

Distributed in the USA by Robin & Russ Handweavers,
533 North Adams Street, McMinnville, Oregon 97128, USA.

This edition
Copyright Ruth Bean, 1984. All rights reserved
ISBN 903585 18 9

Photographs: Pls 1–12 & Fig. 63 Miles Birch, North Bedfordshire
Borough Council; *Frontisp.* & Fig. 38, Koenraad Rutgers.
Designed by James Skelton.
Typeset by Pro-Arts, Wellingborough.
Printed in Great Britain at the University Press Cambridge.

Contents

Foreword to the Translation

Around 1970 my husband bought me a small French book on lace entitled *La dentelle aux fuseaux,* by L. Paulis. It had no cover and no date, but the text was complete, and it was full of very good illustrations. This book has been of great help to me ever since, firstly as a kind of small reference book at a time when such books were almost non-existent, and secondly as an encouragement to start working on my own designs. It has a very matter-of-fact approach to the whole process of lace-making and, although it sets out to describe Cluny lace in particular, much of the text is applicable to all types of lace.

In 1983 I discovered that Ruth Bean, publisher of many books on lace and textiles in general, lived only a few miles away: she saw the book and thought that it was well worth translating. She found out that the book was published in 1921 in Brussels and that Madame Paulis, the author, was later *collaboratrice libre* at the *Musées Royaux d'Art et d'Histoire* there. Among her publications was an important book on the identification of lace, *Pour connaître la dentelle,* 1947.

The text
The text was first translated literally from the French and then transformed into English. Although it follows the original as closely as possible, a number of small changes have been made to bring it up date for the modern lacemaker.

New material in the text is given in square brackets [ ]; round brackets ( ) are used as in the original. New footnotes are indicated by asterisks, daggers etc; the original footnotes are indicated by a number. The French custom of counting the *threads* has been replaced by the English method of counting *pairs*. The *italics* used for emphasis in the original have been retained. A little of the most dated material has been left out, as well as the list of figures. The original figures have been re-traced to reproduce them more clearly. Some completely new material has been added including a chapter on corners.

The lace

All the samples have been re-worked and prickings with notes on their working have been added. Of the twelve pieces in the original, ten were for straight lace, without corners. New corners have been provided for all ten. The photographs show the lace actual size, as in the original, but enlarged photographs of all the corners have been added to show these in greater detail. In the original the plates showing the finished lace were numbered in with the line illustrations as Figures: 2, 38, 53, 63a, 66a and 77. These, together with the new corners, have been renumbered seperately as Plates 1–12 for easier reference.

I would like to thank my husband for the use of his precious word processor and my son Koenraad for his helpful comments. Eunice Arnold for kindly reading the draft translation. Miles Birch for his work and research on the photographs. Ruth and Nigel Bean for their careful scrutiny of the text and for bringing together the many different elements which went into creating this book.

Maria Rutgers, Felmersham, May 1984.

Foreword

This book is written mainly for lace designers. It aims to provide the technical knowledge needed to create designs which can be readily executed, and to prepare prickings if required. It assists lacemakers by explaining systematically the difficulties they may encounter; collectors and others with an interest in lace will find here a way of familiarising themselves with the art of lacemaking without having to devote too much time to it.

The description of pillows, pillow stands, bobbins, pins and various winders has been purposely omitted. Such information may be found in other books on lace.

Introduction

Bobbin lace falls naturally into two groups, each with a very different technique: lace made as a continuous length of fabric and lace made of seperate pieces joined together. Although the laces within one group may look very different, their execution is similar. The subject of this book, Cluny lace, belongs to the first group. Other laces in this group include guipures, Torchon lace, and the various laces with a net background: Valenciennes, Binche, Mechlin, Flemish lace, Chantilly, Lille and Point de Paris.

Before the lacemaker can use a draft design, an accurate pricking must be prepared from it and the position of the pins decided. The pricking is made on coloured cardboard which should be glossy, flexible and strong: coloured parchment would be even better. This is pinned to the pillow, with the footside of the lace to the left*.

A row of pins placed above the top of the pricking will be needed to hold the threads, which may be numerous. The lacemaker is then ready to begin: plaiting, twisting, weaving and crossing the threads in various ways and putting in a pin every time the threads have to be kept in position.

When the lacemaker reaches the bottom of the pricking the pins are carefully removed and the work is lifted and transferred to the top of the pricking. There a sufficient number of pins are re-inserted in the pinholes so that the lace will not be pulled out of shape. Weaving, plaiting, etcetera are then continued, without changing the position of the pillow (Frontisp) †, until the required length is completed.

---

*On the *right,* in the U.K. In my experience when working with a footside on the left the bobbins would be on the right-hand side of the pillow for most of the time. An unspangled bobbin, as they are on the continent, when temporarily laid aside would tend to roll to the right. This would cause an s-twist thread (e.g. cotton) to untwist and hence weaken. A z-twist thread, on the other hand, would become more tightly twisted which would be considered an advantage.

†Today's lacemaker is not restricted to a fixed pillow and can turn her work when required.

PART ONE
Basic Technique

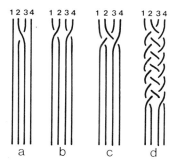

Figure 3
a. A 'cross'. b. A 'twist'. c. A half-stitch. d. A 2-pair plait.

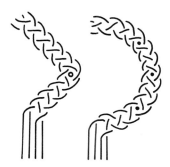

Figure 4
The use of pins to support a curve.

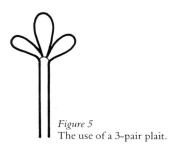

Figure 5
The use of a 3-pair plait.

PLAITS

Cluny lace is made up of plaits which may join, separate or cross in various forms of interlacing. The plaits can be decorated in various ways; they can also be grouped together so that their combined threads form solid *areas*. However, the basic units consist solely of interlacing plaits (Pls 1–4).

The *plaits* or *bars* used most frequently in Cluny lace are made with two pairs. Plaits with one, three or even four pairs are also used. [A plait with only one pair will be called a bar].

Plait with 2 pairs

The four bobbins are hanging on the pillow supported by a pin. Work as follows:

Pick up the second bobbin and place it to the right of the third (1). This is called a *cross* (Fig. 3a). Next, place the second bobbin over the first and the fourth over the third simultaneously. This is called a *twist* (Fig. 3b).

The cross and the twist together form one *half stitch* (Fig. 3c). The 2-pair plait is a succession of half stitches (Fig. 3d).

When the 2-pair plait does not follow a straight line, it must be supported with a pin, whenever it changes direction. The pin is always put in after a half stitch has been completed, i.e. after the twist; and after placing the pin a cross or another half stitch must follow, which has the function of *enclosing the pin*. A curved line must always be supported by at least three pins (Fig. 4).

Plait with 3 pairs

The laces of the 16th century and the beginning of the 17th, which were always heavily starched, often used the motif shown in Figure 5 as edging. The three loops

---

1 Bobbins are always counted from left to right. Their numbering depends not on some earlier position but on their position when the new movement begins. For example, if the second bobbin is placed to the right of the third, it then becomes the third bobbin.

Figure 6
A 3-pair bar.

Figure 7
A 4-pair plait.

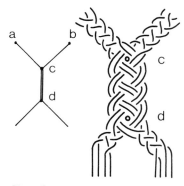

Figure 8
Two 2-pair plaits join to form a 4-pair plait, and then separate again.

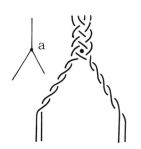

Figure 9
A 2-pair plait separating into two 1-pair bars.

are made with 2-pair plaits, with two threads joining the base. The support plaits must therefore consist of 3 pairs. As a quick way of making a 3-pair plait the lacemaker can work an ordinary plait with three strands, using two bobbins in each strand just as in the 4–pair plait. With 3 pairs hanging from a point (Fig. 6) work as follows:

> Cross the first pair over the second pair; twist the third pair over the second; cross the first pair over the second, and so on…

The same method can be used for a 6-pair plait (very rare), using four bobbins for each movement. Plaits made in this way rarely look good, but perfectly satisfactory results may be obtained using the method explained on page 20.

Plait with 4 pairs

When two plaits of 2 pairs each combine, they form a plait consisting of 4 pairs. The 4-pair plait is, like the 2-pair plait, a succession of half stitches; only two bobbins rather than one are picked up for each movement. (Fig. 7).

To work the pattern in Figure 8, hang two pairs on a pin at *a*, and two on a pin at *b*. On each side, make a plait up to the point where the two lines meet; then begin the 4-pair plait, putting in a pin after the first half stitch. The 4-pair plait continues up to *d* where a pin is put in after the twist. *Enclose* the pin with a *cross* and continue the pattern with two 2-pair plaits.

Bar with 1 pair

Where a single line, representing a 2-pair plait, splits into two lines, they should be worked as bars with one pair each. The 1-pair bar is made by repeating the twist: this twists the two threads, right over left around each other (Fig. 9). A pin is necessary at point *a* to keep the work in shape. This is put in *after* a half stitch: it is enclosed with another half stitch and the twist is then made repeatedly with the right-hand and

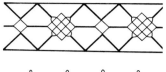

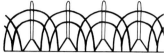

Figure 10
The use of 1-pair bars.

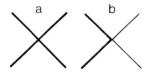

Figure 11
a. Complete crossing. b. Join.

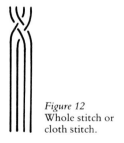

Figure 12
Whole stitch or
cloth stitch.

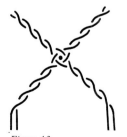

Figure 13
Crossing of two 1-pair bars.

the left-hand pairs. Figure 10 shows examples of 1-pair bars.

Note that the 1-pair bar is not very firm and needs to be well twisted: most lacemakers fail to do this. It is wise to use the 1-pair bar only sparingly, never making it more than 0.5 cm (0.2 in) long.

CROSSINGS

To form a design, the various bars and plaits of Cluny lace must cross each other. Such crossings can be *complete* (when one plait entirely crosses through another) or *incomplete* (Fig. 11). An incomplete crossing is called a *join*: for example, when a plait coming from the left joins a plait to its right then continues to the left.

Four main cases must be considered: 1. A crossing of two plaits, each with the same number of pairs. 2. A crossing of two plaits, each with a different number of pairs. 3. Joins. 4. Multiple crossings.

Crossing two equal plaits

A *whole stitch* consists of a half stitch followed by another cross (Fig. 12). After the whole stitch, the pair which began on the left is on the right and vice versa. The whole stitch is in effect a *crossing* of the two pairs of bobbins.

Crossing two bars with 1 pair each

The two bars are worked up to where they must cross. Then a *whole stitch* is made and each bar is continued (Fig. 13). In general a crossing may be held in place with a pin. The pin is put in, as stated earlier, *after the half stitch*. The exact sequence is then as follows:

> Cross – twist – put in pin – cross – twist left and right to continue the bars.

Windmill crossing (two plaits with 2 pairs each)

This is done as above. The two plaits are worked up to where they must cross. A whole stitch is then made, using two bobbins instead of one for each movement (Fig. 14). The pin which is placed after the half stitch is enclosed with a cross, and the plaiting is continued.

7

Figure 14
Crossing of two 2-pair plaits.

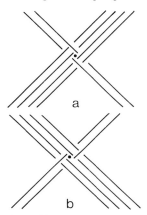

Figure 15
Crossing two unequal bars.

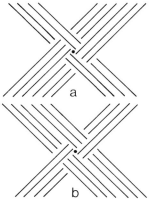

Figure 16
Crossing a 2-pair plait and a 3-pair plait.

Crossing two plaits of 3 pairs each

This is worked as above except that *three bobbins* are used for each movement instead of one or two.

Crossing two plaits of 4 pairs each

This may also be done as above, but with four bobbins for each movement. However, since this is awkward to do, and the result is a little thick, a *join* is usually made instead of a complete crossing.

Crossing two unequal plaits

Sometimes it is necessary to cross a plait with 2 pairs and a plait with 3 pairs, or a bar with 1 pair and a plait with 2 pairs, etc. Such crossings cause no special difficulties. They are worked as *whole stitches;* but for each movement *half* the number of bobbins in each plait is used. Suppose for instance that a bar with 1 pair, coming from the left, must cross a plait with 2 pairs (Fig. 15a) (1).

> Work the bar and plait up to where they cross. There, *cross* one bobbin from the bar with two bobbins from the plait. Then, both on the left and on the right, *twist* two bobbins over one; put in pin and again *cross* one bobbin over two. Continue the bar to the right, and the plait to the left.

When the bar comes from the right, and the plait from the left, work as follows:

> Cross two bobbins over one. Then, on both sides, twist one bobbin over two – put in pin – cross two bobbins over one – continue the bar to the left and the plait to the right.

When a plait with 2 pairs has to cross a plait with 3 pairs work as follows:

> With a 2-pair plait coming from the left (Fig. 16a): cross two bobbins over three – twist three

1 Figures 15 and 16, and a number of other figures, are simplified diagrams. The plaits are represented by parallel lines: one line per thread. This allows the crossing to be understood more easily than with a more detailed figure.

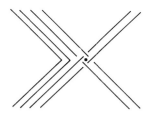

Figure 17
Joining a 2-pair plait and a 1-pair bar.

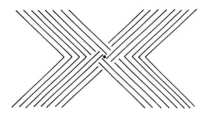

Figure 18
Joining two 4-pair plaits.

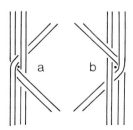

Figure 19
Alternative join of a 2-pair plait and a 1-pair bar, "Fast crossing".

bobbins over two – put in pin – cross two bobbins over three. With a 2-pair plait coming from the right (Fig. 16b): cross three bobbins over two – twist two bobbins over three – put in pin – cross three bobbins over two.

Joins

Joins are made between unequal plaits, as shown in Figure 11b, but a crossing of two plaits with 4 pairs each is an exception, for which see below.

Generally, when two unequal plaits are to be joined, a crossing is worked, using only the number of pairs from the larger plait that is in the smaller plait. The remaining pairs of the larger plait are temporarily laid aside. After completing the crossing, each plait is continued in its own direction.

Suppose, for instance, that a plait with 2 pairs and a bar with 1 pair are to be joined (Fig. 17). A crossing is worked as if two bars consisting of 1 pair each were involved without using the left-hand pair of the plait. After completing the crossing, the plait is continued to the left, and the bar to the right.

In the special case where two plaits with 4 pairs each are joined (Fig. 18), the crossing is worked as if two 2-pair plaits were involved. Half the pairs in each plait are laid aside for the moment. After completing the crossing, the two 4-pair plaits are continued.

Fast crossing

When a pattern requires a bar with 1 pair to join a plait with 2 pairs, the lacemaker may wish to make a *fast crossing* as explained below, which is firm, quick to make, and *very* neat:

a. 1-pair bar coming from the right (Fig. 19a). Cross the second pair from the plait over the pair of the bar – twist the second pair over the first – put in pin between the second and third pairs – enclose the pin by crossing the second pair over the third. In other words: with two bobbins in each hand, work a 4-pair crossing without the fourth pair.

9

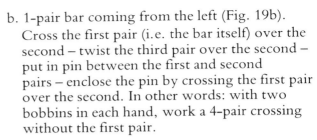

b. 1-pair bar coming from the left (Fig. 19b).
Cross the first pair (i.e. the bar itself) over the
second – twist the third pair over the second –
put in pin between the first and second
pairs – enclose the pin by crossing the first pair
over the second. In other words: with two
bobbins in each hand, work a 4-pair crossing
without the first pair.

Multiple crossings
Crossing three plaits

This crossing most frequently looks like the
arrangement in Figure 20a. However, the plaits may
take quite different directions, both before and after
the crossing, as in Figs. 20b and 20c. The crossing may
be worked in several ways:

Method I (Fig. 21a)

The middle plait does not take part in this
crossing. With plaits 2 and 3 work a half
stitch – put in pin in the centre of *all* the threads,
i.e. between the sixth bobbin and the seventh
bobbin. Then, lift the 2 pairs of the centre plait
with the left hand, and complete the whole stitch
with the other hand. Put back the bobbins of the
centre plait and continue working each of the
three plaits as before.

This crossing, fast and easy though it is, has the
shortcoming of not being securely fixed. After the pin
is taken out, it may slide on the centre pair which runs
straight through the crossing. When a fixed crossing is
needed, the second method should be used.

Method II (Fig. 21b)

Before starting the crossing, lift the right-hand
pair of the centre plait with one hand. With the
other hand work the crossing as in Method I up to
putting in the pin. After the pin is in place, put
back the pair held in one hand to the right of the
pin. Then lift the other pair of the centre plait
(lying to the left of the pin) and complete the
whole stitch, working *under* the lifted pair, and

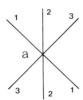

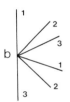

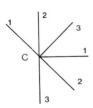

Figure 20
Crossing of three plaits.

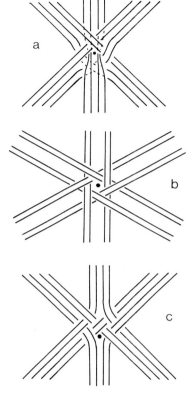

Figure 21
Three ways to work a 3-plait crossing.

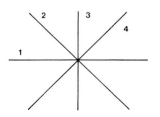

Figure 22
Crossing of four plaits.

over the pair just put back. The three plaits are each continued as before. This crossing is firm and very neat.

Method III (Fig. 21c)

Work the three plaits up to where they are to cross, and lay them down, side by side. Then cross pair 2 over pair 3, and pair 4 over pair 5. Twist pair 2 over pair 1, pair 4 over pair 3 and pair 6 over pair 5. Put a pin in the middle of all the threads. Cross pair 2 over pair 3 again, and pair 4 over pair 5. Continue with the three plaits as before. This crossing is easy to do, but not as neat and firm as the one above.

The three meeting plaits need not have 2 pairs each. The movements of the crossing do not change, however unequal the plaits. What does change is the number of bobbins picked up for each movement.

Crossing four plaits

This usually looks like the diagram in Figure 22 and is worked as follows:

Make the plaits up to the point where they cross, and then work with plaits 2, 3 and 4 according to Method I for a 3-plait crossing, up to putting in the pin. That is: leave plait 3 hanging, and make a half stitch with plaits 2 and 4 – putting the pin in the centre of the three pairs.

Next, work a whole stitch with plait 1 and the 6 pairs of plaits 2, 3 and 4, thus: *cross* two bobbins from plait 1 over six bobbins from the remaining plaits – *twist* each group of six bobbins over two bobbins of plait 1 – remove pin, and replace it in the centre of the whole stitch now being made. Finish the whole stitch by *crossing* the second pair of plait 1 over the right-hand group of six bobbins. Plait 1 may now be continued, and the crossing finished according to Method I for the three plaits, by lifting the bobbins of the third plait and crossing pair 2 over 3. The remaining three plaits may then also be continued.

When plait 1 passes through the crossing from right to left, the whole stitch with the 6 pairs of plaits 2, 3 and 4, and the two pairs of plait 1 is now worked as follows: cross six bobbins over two, twist two bobbins over six, put in pin, cross six bobbins over two. The rest of the crossing remains unchanged.

Crossing five plaits

This crossing often resembles Figure 23a. Plait 1, after having crossed the three other plaits, comes back as plait 5. So, while plait 1 crosses from left to right, plait 5 crosses from right to left. This crossing is worked like the preceding one as far as plaits 1, 2, 3 and 4 are concerned, i.e. like a 4-plait crossing. The difference is that, having taken plait 1 up to *a* and back to the crossing (as plait 5), work another whole stitch with this plait and the twelve bobbins of plaits 2, 3 and 4.

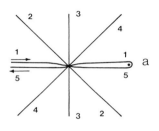

Detailed explanation of the second whole stitch: Cross the right-hand group of six bobbins over the first pair of plait 5. Twist the two pairs of plait 5 over the two groups of six bobbins – remove the pin and put it back in the centre of the whole stitch which is being made – finish the whole stitch by crossing six bobbins over the second pair of the plait.

Plait 5 may now be continued. The crossing is completed in the same way as the 3- and 4-plait crossings.

If plait 1 comes from the right and plait 5 form the left, the method is the same. Only the whole stitches made with plaits 2, 3 and 4 and plait 1, and then with plait 5 must be worked in the opposite direction.

When the crossing of five plaits resembles Figure 23b (1), it is made as follows: With plaits 2, 3 and 4 work a crossing of three plaits, using Method I, up to putting in the pin. Then, with plaits 1 and 5 make an

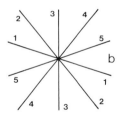

Figure 23
Crossing of five plaits.
b. Alternative arrangement of the five plaits.

---

1 Details for working this crossing, and the crossing in Figure 27a, have been given by Miss Diane van Houtte, teacher at the lace school in Bruges.

ordinary crossing of two plaits, partly above and partly below the other plaits.

In detail: cross – twist, leaving the other twelve bobbins where they are, – take out pin, and put it back in the centre of *all* the threads – lift and hold the twelve bobbins and complete the crossing; then put the twelve bobbins down again. Finish the 3-pair crossing of plaits 2, 3 and 4 according to Method I.

Crossings of more than five plaits at one point may also occur. The large number of threads prevents a neat solution, and the work becomes very complicated. It would be better to replace such crossings with small areas of clothwork, as explained in Part Two.

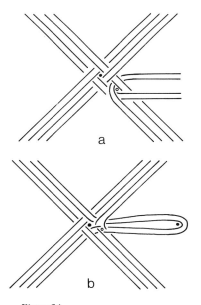

Figure 24
A 1-pair bar connected to a crossing of two plaits. a. A bar approaching the crossing and leaving again. b. A bar leaving and returning to a crossing.

Other crossings
Crossings with a 1-pair bar

Sometimes a 1-pair bar must connect with a crossing of two or three plaits.

a. A 1-pair bar connected to a crossing of two plaits. (Fig. 24a)

First a windmill crossing is made with the two plaits; then, with the 1-pair bar and the plait next to it, work a fast crossing as shown in Figure 19. The pin used to support the first crossing is taken out, but put back in the same place to support the new crossing as well.

b. A 1-pair bar connected to a crossing of three plaits.

The procedure is the same as in *a* above. The second crossing is also made in the same way; then the pin is taken out and put back again as above. It is advisable to start the second crossing only after the plaits not needed to work it have been completed.

If instead of approaching the crossing and leaving it again, the 1-pair bar *leaves* the crossing and then comes back, the following procedure should be adopted.

c. A 1-pair bar leaving and returning to a 2-plait crossing.

The first half of the crossing is made as in *a* above: cross – twist – put in pin. Figure 24b illustrates the case where the extreme right pair will form the 1-pair bar which leaves the crossing and comes back. With the pair of the bar, and the pair closest to it, work a whole stitch and support it with the same pin. Here, too, the pin is used twice. Finally the first crossing is completed, as always, with a cross.

If three plaits instead of two meet at the crossing, the procedure is the same. That is:

Work a crossing (p. 10) with three plaits up to putting in the pin; form the 1-pair bar, bring it back and make a whole stitch with the pair closest to it; support the whole stitch with the same pin; and finally complete the crossing of the three plaits.

Crossings at the footside (Fig. 25)

As a rule, lace has a kind of *selvedge* on the footside, which prevents it from being stretched or pulled out of shape. This selvedge is occasionally replaced by a simple 1-pair bar. In order to keep the edge firm it is better *not* to make *complete crossings* when other bars or plaits are connected to the 1-pair bar. The following crossings could be worked instead.

When a 1-pair bar at the footside needs to be connected to another 1-pair bar, work as follows:

Cross – twist *twice* – put in pin – cross – continue the two bars. The second twist causes threads *a* to return to the body of the lace, and threads *b* to remain in a straight line.

When the footside is formed by a 2-pair plait, an incomplete crossing or join must be made every time another bar or plait is connected to it. In this way, out of the four threads making up the footside, only two change direction and the other two ensure the firmness of the lace.

Figure 25
Crossing at the footside.

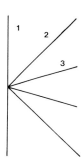

Figure 26
Multiple crossing at the footside.

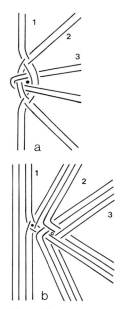

Figure 27
Two multiple crossings at the footside. a. Three 1-pair bars. b. Three 2-pair plaits.

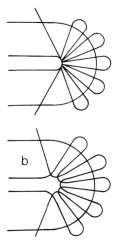

Figure 28
Crossings accumulated at one point.

Sometimes several bars meet at the same point on the footside (Fig. 26). In the case of three 1-pair bars (Fig. 27a) work as follows:

Work a whole stitch with bars 1 and 2; make a crossing with the two pairs of these two bars and the pair of the third bar, picking up two bobbins for each movement; put in pin as indicated in the Figure. Return bar 3 back into the lace, as follows: cross pair 2 over pair 3 – twist pairs 1 and 2 twice – put in pin – cross pair 2 over pair 3. This rather long but very firm crossing is completed by another whole stitch with pairs 1 and 2.

In the case of 2-pair plaits crossing at the footside (Fig. 27b), make a join with plaits 1 and 2, i.e. work a whole stitch with the right-hand pair of plait 1 and the left-hand pair of plait 2; then work a windmill crossing with plaits 2 and 3. Remove the pin which first supported the join and put it back in to support the second crossing.

In the case of unequal plaits: for example if plait 3 is a 1-pair bar approaching and leaving the footside at a right angle (this happens very often), the procedure is similar to that shown in Figure 24a, page 13. The only difference is that the first crossing is replaced by a join, to preserve the firmness of the footside. The same applies when the bar leaves the footside and then returns to it (Fig. 24b).

The working of multiple crossings presents the greatest technical problem in Cluny lace. It cannot be overemphasized that the threads must be pulled up very firmly around the pins, to keep the work accurate and firm.

The designer must not use complicated crossings too freely. Close repetition of simple crossings must also be avoided because they will detract from the appearance of the lace, unless perfectly made. Figure 28 is an example of such accumulated crossings, which are time-consuming and tiresome to do. Figure 28b

15

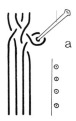

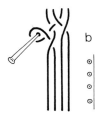

Figure 29
Simple picots.

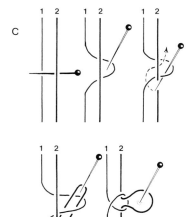

Figure 29
Knotted picots.

shows in detail the course of each plait★. The extreme closeness of the crossings prevents their being supported by one pin each. The same pinhole is, in this case, used six[†] times.

PICOTS

The plaits in Cluny lace are often decorated with *picots*. The picots may be placed at the right- or left-hand side of the plait, or both. They are made by twisting one thread of the plait around a pin[‡].

Picot made on the right of a plait (Fig. 29a)

The plait is worked up to where a picot is marked on the pattern. Place the pin *under* the extreme right thread of the plait, pointing downwards and to the left. Pass the tip of the pin [anti-clockwise] *over* this thread and insert it into the pinhole. Twist the right-hand pair once and continue working the plait.

Picot made on the left of a plait (Fig. 29b)

Place the pin *under* the extreme left thread of the plait, pointing upwards and to the right. Pass the tip [again anti-clockwise] *over* the thread and insert it into the pinhole. Twist the left-hand pair once and continue the plait. You can start with the pin pointing down- and inwards, but the above method is easier.

When several picots follow each other on the same side of a plait, it is better to work them all with the same thread. This thread will be on the same side

★ In an arrangement such as that illustrated in Figure 28 there are long loops at the headside made entirely with one plait. Such patterns should be worked only with linen (s-twist) thread, otherwise the plaits will cork-screw. (See detail in Pl. 1)

† The original reads three. However, the translator after working the pattern, concludes this should read six.

‡ Note, however, that this old-fashioned picot is only possible with linen (s-twist) thread. This was pointed out by Mrs Claire Burkhard of Turgi, Switzerland, 1984.

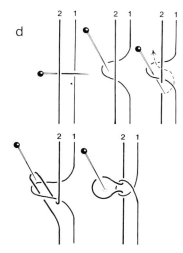

d

again, and ready for the next picot after the cross has been made twice.

Knotted picots (Fig. 29 c–d) ★

The simple picots illustrated in Figures 29a and b may be succesfully replaced with the versions in Figures 29c and d. To make them, work as follows:

> Place the pin *under* thread *2* and over thread *1* – pull thread *1* under thread *2* – place the tip of the pin over thread *2* and move the tip of the pin upwards as indicated by the arrow – pull thread *2* through (this loop will be the picot) and insert the pin into the pinhole – pull up both threads carefully. If you are making the picot on a plait, twist the other pair once before continuing.

You will find that the right–hand picot fits in better than the left–hand version. Therefore, if you are making a pattern with many picots on the headside it is better to put the pricking on your pillow with the headside to the right.

A plait with staggered picots, called in French: *tresse mignardise* is shown in Figure 38.

Figure 29
Knotted picots (continued).

Figure 30
Plait with staggered picots, *tresse mignardise*.

VENETIAN BARS

Venetian bars *(bride de Venise)* are usually made from two thick threads, covered by a finer lace thread. This third thread passes alternately over and under the thick threads.

When the fine thread starts at the right of the two thick ones (Fig. 31) work as follows:

> Twist the fine thread over thick thread *2*. Pass thick thread *1* over the fine thread, and the fine thread over the same thick thread, i.e. cross twice. Pass thick thread *2* over the fine thread and the fine thread over the same thick thread, i.e. twist twice. Continue in the same way: cross twice, twist twice, etc. The fine thread must be pulled up very carefully and the weaving movements must

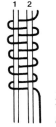

Figure 31
Venetian bar,
bride de Venise.

★ Figure and text new to this edition.

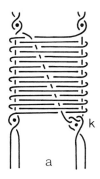

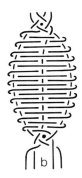

Figure 32
Tallies, *points d'esprit*.

be repeated as often as necessary to form a very regular and compact braid.

When a Venetian bar is part of a crossing, the fine thread is combined with one of the thick threads, and the Venetian bar is treated as an ordinary 1-pair bar. Sometimes the Venetian bar is made by replacing each of the thick threads by two ordinary lace threads.

LEADWORK or TALLIES

The working of a tally *(point d'esprit)* is similar to that of a Venetian bar. It is usually made with four threads. One of these runs from right to left and back again, passing alternately over and under each of the three other threads. The two outer threads determine the shape of the tally, which may be square, oval or triangular.

Square tally (Fig. 32a)

One pair is supported by a pin at each of the two upper corners of the square. Starting from the right, work as follows:

> Cross the second bobbin over the third – twist the left pair twice – cross the second bobbin over the third – twist the right pair twice – and so on.

The two threads which determine the shape of the tally must be kept taut at all times. When the tally is finished, a pin is put in each of the two lower corners of the square and each pin again supports two threads. To secure the tally a single knot is made, as shown in the Figure. Take care *not* to use the weaver when making the knot.

Oval tally or 'leaf' (Fig.32b)

This shape is very common in Cluny lace. The leaf is started with a whole stitch, supported by a pin, and continued as explained above. The two outer threads are kept well apart for the first half of the tally and then gradually brought closer. The leaf is finished with another whole stitch, supported by a pin.

Triangular tally (Fig. 32c)

A triangular tally may have its point at the top or at the bottom. The method is similar to that of the preceding tallies. When the point is at the bottom, the beginning is like that of the square tally. When the point is at the top, the beginning is like that of the oval tally, and the end is like that of the square tally. Two triangular tallies may be worked one after the other, and joined at the point.

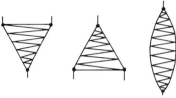   

b

Figure 33
How to indicate tallies on a pattern.

Finally there are tallies consisting of six or eight threads. They are time-consuming and difficult to make and it is advisable to keep them in shape with a few extra pins (Fig. 33b). Note, that a tally must never cross a plait.

Tallies should be inked in on the pricking as indicated in Figure 33.

CLOTHWORK

Cluny lace does not always consist of intersecting plaits alone, but may have solid areas as well. These are formed by combining the threads from two or more plaits, spreading them out side by side and weaving them together into a small area of true clothwork.

Two of the available threads form the weft of the cloth stitch area, travelling from right to left and back again, alternately over and under each of the other threads. The two weft threads are called the *weavers (voyageurs)*. As a rule, when the weavers have reached the edge of the cloth stitch area, they are twisted once or twice, and passed around a pin which is needed to support them. In this way they form a series of small loops at both edges.

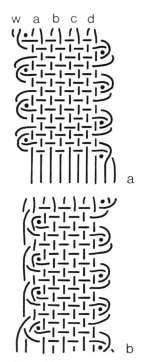

w a b c d

a

b

Figure 34
Cloth stitch areas. a. With small
loops on both sides. b. With small
loops on one side only.

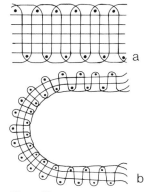

a

b

Figure 35
Clothwork areas with an exchange
of weavers. Each line represents
one pair of threads.

Suppose, for example, that a cloth stitch area is to be formed with ten threads (from two 2-pair plaits and a 1-pair bar) (Fig. 34a). Work as follows:

one cloth stitch with the first pair *w,* being the weavers, and the second pair *a* – one cloth stitch with the weavers and pair *b* – one cloth stitch with the weavers and pair *c* – and one cloth stitch with the weavers and pair *d*. Twist the weavers once or twice and put in pin. Then one cloth stitch with the weavers and pair *d* – one cloth stitch with the weavers and pair *c,* and so on to the left-hand edge. Twist the weavers once or twice, put in the pin and work again from left to right with cloth stitches through the warp threads or passive pairs.

Sometimes only one edge has the small loops, while the other is plain. Works as follows (Fig. 34b).

When the weavers, coming from the right, have crossed the last pair on the left, leave them. The pair of warp threads just passed through becomes a weaver pair instead. Work the small loop on the right as before. When the new weavers have worked their way back to the left again, leave them in turn, and replace them by the pair just passed through (i.e. the old weavers). Continue working in this way.

Note that when two pairs of weavers change places in this way, the pin must *not* be placed in the centre of the cloth stitch, but to one side of it after the cloth stitch has been completed. This will keep the new weavers in place.

The weavers may *change places* on both sides of a cloth work area. The process is shown in Figure 35a where *each line represents two threads.* The narrowest cloth work that can be made in this way has only 3 pairs. It looks just like a plait (1), and in well executed lace it should replace the simple 3-pair plait described earlier, on page 6.

1. Made *without pins*.

20

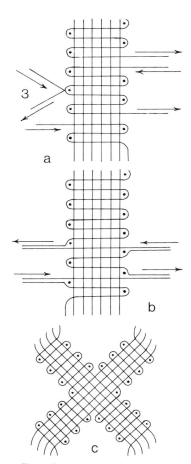

Figure 36
Exchange of weavers applied to various situations.

On the inside of a curve the small loops are generally left out. Figure 35b shows the proper arrangement of the threads. The curve may of course also be drawn the other way round. It is not strictly necessary to use pins on the *inside* of the curve. An experienced lacemaker will pull up the warp threads at the right moment and so keep the weavers in place when they change over, without needing any pins.

The exchange of weaver pairs plays an important part in the working of cloth stitch areas. It is used in all the detailed descriptions below.

a. When a weaver pair is needed elsewhere, it leaves the clothwork area and is immediately replaced by another pair, as shown in Figure 36a. In this figure, and in all succeeding figures, *one line represents two threads*.

b. When a plait crosses a clothwork area (Fig. 36b), the weavers are laid aside at the point where the new plait is to emerge. One of the two pairs of the incoming plait will pass straight through in a series of cloth stitches. Together with the old weavers it will form the new plait. The remaining pair of the plait becomes the new weaver pair.

c. Sometimes a plait must be connected to a clothwork area. When this happens the fast crossing explained on page 9, could be made, or a join, using one pair from the plait, regardless of the number of pairs it contains, and the weavers from the clothwork. In either case the weavers will be replaced by another pair.

d. When two clothwork areas cross each other, the warp threads of one area are worked through the warp threads of the other in a series of cloth stitches. The two weaver pairs change direction as shown in Figure 36c.

e. A clothwork area may be reduced or enlarged by leaving out pairs or adding new ones. In both cases the clothwork must remain quite regular and its outline maintained.

Figure 37a shows two pairs leaving a band of clothwork. The dotted line indicates the outline which has to be followed.

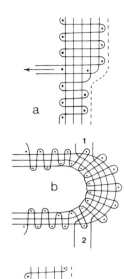

Figure 37
Adding and removing pairs from
clothwork.

Figure 38
Reproduction of an old lace design.
Note the accumulation of pairs at
the footside.

In Figure 37b a crescent-shaped area of clothwork is expanded by adding threads at *1* and taking them out again at *2*.

Some old pieces of lace have very dense, shapeless areas at the footside, where a large number of threads accumulate between two scallops (Fig. 38 and Pls. 5a–b). The function of these dense areas is to temporarily suppress the threads which cannot be used in the lace. They are sometimes unavoidable, but their use proves that the design is not perfectly suited to the technique. In good designs the threads are used all the time in interesting ways, and technical constraints must be studied and exploited for ornament if possible. This means always seeing ahead in order to create a beautiful result.

As far as clothwork is concerned, the area it will occupy must be indicated as precisely as possible. The threads which compose it must be drawn in some detail as in the accompanying figures.

In particular, showing the course of the weavers will give the lacemaker the best possible guidance. Furthermore, the preparation of the pricking *requires* this kind of detailed drawing, otherwise it is impossible to determine where the pinholes should be.

RAISED WORK

In some laces special tallies are used on a cloth stitch background and giving a relief effect. This is achieved as follows:

> Work the cloth stitch just up to the point where the raised work is to start. Then make the tally with two of the warp pairs, explained in the section on tallies, p 18. Lay the two pairs used for the tally well to one side, supported by a pin. Continue the clothwork up to the point where the tally comes back into the work. Then lay the two pairs back in place, and continue the work.

TWISTED CLOTH STITCH

A twisted cloth stitch is made (Fig. 39) by twisting the pairs again after an ordinary cloth stitch. Twisted cloth stitches play an important part in plaited lace. They can form an open fabric which looks more attractive than ordinary cloth stitch. It is done as follows (Fig. 39a):

> Work a twisted cloth stitch with pairs 1 and 2 (the first pair is the weaver pair) – a twisted cloth stitch with the weavers and the next pair – a twisted cloth stitch with the weavers and each of the following pairs. After the last twisted cloth stitch put in pin, twist the weavers once more, and then start working back.

A straight edge, without the small loops, may be obtained by exchanging the weavers, as explained earlier for ordinary cloth stitch, p 20 and Figure 34b.

It is also possible to make twisted cloth stitch areas

Figure 39
Twisted cloth stitch.

Figure 39a
An area of twisted cloth stitches.

23

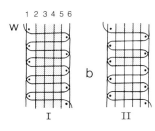

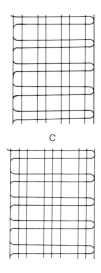

Figure 40
Working diagrams for twisted cloth stitches.

with the pairs running at an angle, between two straight edges. This is shown in Figure 40a, and worked as follows:

> Work a twisted cloth stitch with pairs 1 and 2 – with pairs 3 and 4 – with pairs 2 and 3 – and with pairs 2 and 1 – put in pin. Then work a twisted cloth stitch with pairs 5 and 6 – with pairs 4 and 5 – with pairs 3 and 4 – with pairs 2 and 3 – with pairs 1 and 2 – put in pin. Then a twisted cloth stitch with pairs 6 and 7 – put in pin. Continue with a twisted cloth stitch with pairs 5 and 6 – pairs 4 and 5 – and so on.

After reaching the left-hand edge, when the pin is in place, leave the bobbins and start a new row from the right-hand edge. It will be clear from the diagram when the pins must be put in, and also that each pin must be placed on the *inside* of the two pairs which form the twisted cloth stitch at the edges. It is better to give the pairs forming the edges an extra twist, i.e. the extreme right-hand pair *before* a new row is started, and the extreme left-hand pair *after* the last twisted cloth stitch of each row is completed.

When working longer rows, or to obtain very even work or, in fact, whenever it seems necessary, *every* twisted cloth stitch may be supported by a pin. The pin may be placed in the middle of the stitch, or after the stitch has been completed, whichever serves best to support it.

Any plain cloth stitch area may be transformed entirely into twisted cloth stitch, or broken up with a row of twisted cloth stitch; it may even be given a border of twisted cloth stitch. The course of the work remains the same in all cases. In the diagrams of Figure 40b, the ordinary cloth stitch areas are shaded, while the twisted cloth stitch areas are drawn as lines only.

Proceed by following diagram 40b (I):

> Work a twisted cloth stitch with pair *w* and the first pair next to it – a cloth stitch with the weavers and pairs 2, 3, 4, and 5 – *twist the weavers* – a twisted cloth stitch with the weavers and pair

6 – put in pin (!) – a cloth stitch with the *new* weavers and pairs 5, 4, 3, 2, – *twist the weavers* – a twisted cloth stitch with the weavers and pair 1 – put in pin, and so on.

The edges will be firmer if the pairs forming them are given a second twist.

To work diagram 40b (II) proceed as follows:

Work a twisted cloth stitch with pair *w* and the first pair next to it – a cloth stitch with the weavers and pairs 2, 3, 4, and 5 – *twist the weavers* – a twisted cloth stitch with the weavers and pair 6 – put in pin – *twist pairs 2, 3, 4, and 5 once,* then make with these and the weavers a series of twisted cloth stitches. The twisted cloth stitches may be supported by a pin if necessary. Work a twisted cloth stitch with the weavers and pair 1 – put in pin – a series of *ordinary* cloth stitches with the weavers and pairs 2, 3, 4, and 5 – twist the weavers – a twisted cloth stitch with the weavers and the last pair on the right. Continue by following the diagram.

Here too, it is better to give the pairs which form the footside an extra twist.

The work is not difficult but be careful to *twist* the threads *before* the first twisted cloth stitch of the edge, and *before* the row of twisted cloth stitch, in order to seperate them from the ordinary clothwork.

With the same number of bobbins an area of twisted cloth stitch may cover a larger surface than an area of ordinary cloth stitch. This is because the twisted cloth stitches can easily be spaced out a little without spoiling the appearance of the lace. It is even possible to twist the pairs two or three times between stitches. By combining single and multiple twists, interesting lattice effects can be obtained (Fig. 40c).

Note that all these patterns may also be worked at an angle to the footside.

The order of working twisted cloth stitch is the same as for ordinary cloth stitch, which has already been explained. The reader should refer to the section on adding and leaving out pairs, plaits crossing through or joining clothwork, etc. p. 19, remembering the importance of inking in the exact course of the pairs on the pricking.

SPIDERS

A spider is a decorative crossing of several 1-pair bars; the motif is worked in cloth stitch and can be oval or round. The spider may be large or small, depending on the number of pairs available. The simplest spiders are made according to Figure 41a or b. Naturally, a larger number of pairs can be used (Fig. 41c).

Variations d and e have a decorative hole in the centre. If a bigger hole is required to enlarge the area of the motif, this can be done as in Figure 41f. The centre pairs are carried to the outer edges of the motif, secured with a pin, and taken back again to the middle. There, an exchange of weavers takes place as indicated in the figure. The second half is worked like the first half.

A spider surrounded by a row of twisted cloth stitch, made with two additional pairs, is called a 'haloed' spider *(araignée cerclée)*.

Spiders are most frequently supported by a single pin, placed *in the centre* of the motif. When the spider is rather large, it is better to use a pin at the top and the bottom of the motif as well, as indicated in Figure 41. Any twisted cloth stitches surrounding the spider must each be kept firmly in place with a pin.

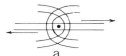

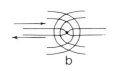

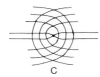

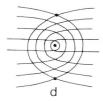

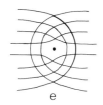

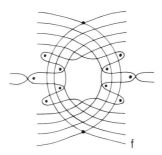

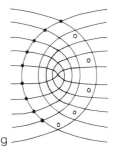

Figure 41
The spiders. The left- and right-hand sides of diagram g show two alternative ways of placing the pins.

26

PART TWO

The Study of Old Lace Designs

EXAMPLES FROM HISTORIC LACE

The study of historic lace makes it easier to appreciate the possibilities of the various basic techniques. Examples of both simple and elaborate motifs may be used either as they are or with modifications.

Detailed drawings will be provided rather than long explanations for laces which may pose special difficulties. By examining these drawings in detail, both lacemakers and designers will gain sufficient understanding of the technique to carry out their work.

The technique has been taken from examples of old lace, most of which are in the collection of the Musée du Cinquantenaire in Brussels.

Four basic shapes have been distinguished: lines, crossings, circular motifs, and scallops or pointed motifs.

Decorated Lines

Decorated lines usually consist of interlacing bars or plaits, running between two parallel bars (Fig. 42: 1 – 4). These bars may be doubled (Fig. 42: 5 – 8). Short lines at right angles to the supporting bars are obtained by a series of crossings (Fig. 42: 9 and 10). Interesting variations of the last two examples are shown in 11, 12,

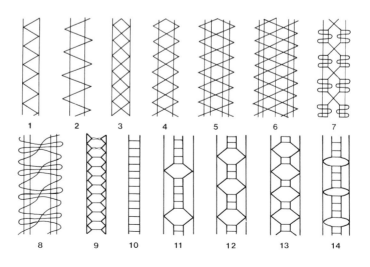

Figure 42
Decorated lines.

27

and 13. Variation 14 is obtained by replacing the squares by less open shapes.

The crossing of three plaits shown in Figure 43s may be elaborated to give the motifs in 1, 2, and 3 of the same Figure. These different crossings will be described in the next section, although their execution should be clear from the diagrams.

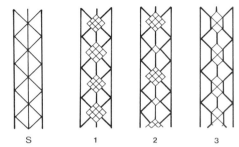

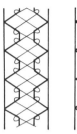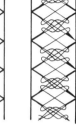

Figure 43
Decorated lines.

Figure 44
Decorated lines.

The two decorated lines shown in Figure 44 have the same general layout. They are different, in that the centre plait has been replaced by two 1-pair bars. The second example, in which the main crossing has been formed out of ordinary whole stitches, instead of the twisted whole stitches used before, is particularly successful.

The special crossings called spiders may also be used to create a large variety of lines. Small simple spiders

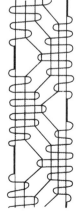

Figure 46
A decorated line.

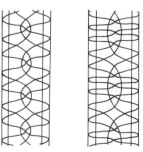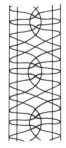

Figure 45
Decorated lines.

28

may be used in succession; they may be elongated by repeating the centre crossing once or twice; or they may be alternated with different crossings (Fig. 45).

The lines may be decorated with a mixture of cloth-work and bars without losing the character of Cluny lace, provided that the solid parts do not dominate the open areas. Figure 46 is a very attractive example.

The majority of decorated lines take the form of narrow insertions, which were often used for underwear to replace the much more costly needle-made drawn work. Some may be used to replace the foot-side, normally formed by a row of twisted cloth stitches next to a cloth stitch band of four passives. Finally, they are used as interesting decorative elements in themselves (See Part Three, page 34).

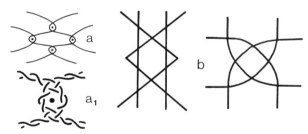

Figure 47
Decorated crossings. a. Crossing of four 1-pair bars. a1. Detail.
b. Crossing of four 2-pair plaits.

Decorated crossings

Crossings of two or more bars are often transformed into motifs. These motifs may simply result from a more interesting arrangement of the bars (Fig. 47). Generally however, the threads are spread out to form a solid area. They are woven together with cloth stitches or twisted cloth stitches, or a combination of both.

The simplest of these modified crossings is worked entirely in cloth stitch. With an *even* number of plaits this will not cause any difficulties (Fig. 48a). With an *odd* number of plaits the crossing is worked according to Figure 48b. All such crossings form square shapes. A rounded shape may be obtained when the crossings are transformed into spiders.

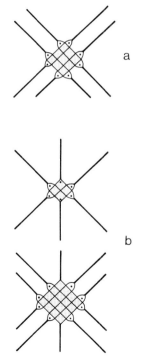

Figure 48
Crossings worked in cloth stitch.

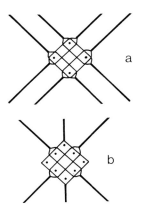

Figure 49
Crossings worked in twisted cloth stitch.

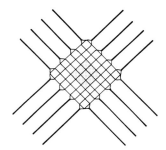

Figure 50
Decorated crossings. Combination of ordinary and twisted cloth stitches.

The crossing shown in Figure 48 may also be worked in twisted cloth stitch. The course of the work remains the same. When coarse thread is used, it is better to support each crossing at the edge with a pin; in all other cases it is sufficient to have a pin at every other stitch (Fig. 49a).

A crossing of three plaits is a little fuller and is better defined when worked in twisted cloth stitch as in Figure 49b.

When the number of plaits is large enough, it is possible to create a variety of different crossings, by combining ordinary cloth stitch, twisted cloth stitch, and even plaits. Figure 50 offers some examples. The plain cloth stitches are shaded to distinguish them from the twisted cloth stitches. These crossings are usually square-shaped.

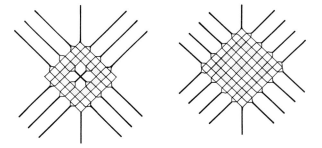

There are also quite different types of crossings, which are less obvious. They are characterised by the way in which the threads are spread out, thereby lightening an otherwise heavy arrangement. The first of these motifs is made with one 2-pair plait and two 1-pair bars (Fig. 51). If there were three 2-pair plaits, some crossings would be replaced by joins. Obviously, this kind of arrangement is not as stable. The three decorated crossings in Figure 52 form different shapes, and are all open.

In narrow laces, the decorated crossings serve to break the monotony of the lines, as in Plates 6 – 8. In some laces they form the main feature like a kind of lattice.

30

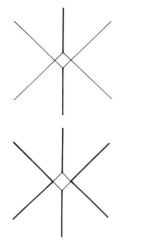

Figure 51
Other crossings.

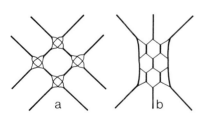

Figure 52
Other crossings with three and four plaits.

Circular motifs

One of the greatest technical problems encountered with Cluny lace is that the lacemaker *cannot easily work upwards*. Plaiting and weaving should proceed only downwards, either vertically or at an angle. To work a line slanting upwards is always very difficult. This problem becomes particularly obvious when a circular shape has to be worked.

The only solution is to proceed according to Figure 54a. The circle is started at *1*, where at least one pair must be laid aside to subsequently close the circle. Up to *2* the work proceeds upwards, and is therefore very awkward; the same is true between *3* and *4*. At point *4* the pair laid aside earlier is taken up again, and added to the other pairs. Circular motifs which are treated in this way occur very often in old lace. Nevertheless, they represent defects in design.

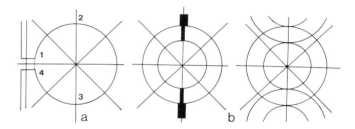

Figure 54
Three ways of forming a circular motif.

It is very much simpler to think of the circle as being composed of two semi-circles, placed symmetrically on each side of a vertical line (Fig. 54b). The pairs start together in one group, and then seperate into two halves: one going to the right, and the other to the left. They each describe a semi-circle and then recombine into one group. This kind of motif always needs additional pairs running straight through to make the shape stable.

Figure 55 shows a series of motifs taken from old lace. In *a* the work is very simple, with ordinary 2-pair plaits for the circles. In *b* the plaits have been replaced

31

Figure 55
Motifs from old lace. a–b. Circular
motifs. c. Motifs which may be
inscribed within a circle.

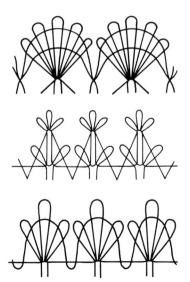

Figure 56
Scallops consisting of plaited loops.

by decorated lines. Almost all the crossings have been
transformed into ornamental motifs. The motifs in *c*
have the same general shape as the preceding motifs, or
may be inscribed within a circle.

Scallops and pointed motifs

The working of scallops and related shapes is particularly difficult because the same number of threads
must be used throughout the lace, without cutting
them, or adding to them.

In old lace the scalloped edge often seems out of
place in relation to the design it is supposed to border.
The examples in Figure 56 are all based on the same
basic loop which is repeated several times, forming a
kind of palm shape.

A great many motifs are constructed along these
lines, with one loop next to the other (Fig. 57). They
are difficult to make, because many crossings come
together at one point, and also because it will be
necessary to *work upwards*. In addition they lack
stability. For these reasons they are generally rather
impractical.

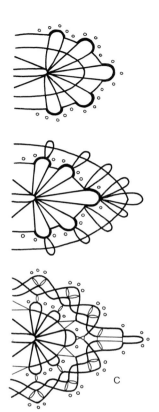

Although scallops derived from old lace are of little practical value nowadays, it is still possible to extract some useful ideas from them. Figure 58 shows in detail a motif based on the preceding figures, but here successfully transformed.

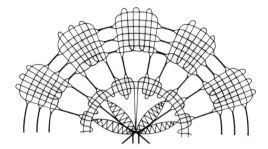

Figure 58
Motif with clothwork.

The motifs in Figure 59 have been taken from Italian laces, and show two interesting ways of working pointed shapes. Finally the idea of surrounding a scallop with a decorated line may lead to excellent results (Fig. 57c).

Figure 57
Scallops consisting of plaited loops.
c. A scallop surrounded by a decorated line.

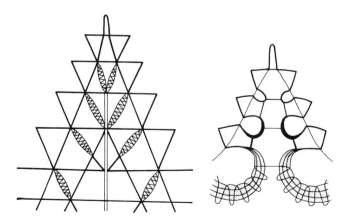

Figure 59
Pointed motifs, taken from Italian laces.

PART THREE
Composition And Design

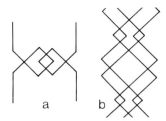

Figure 60
Interlacings. a. Impossible;
b. possible interlacings.

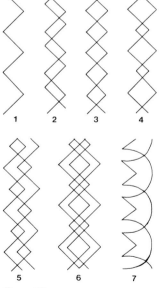

Figure 62
1. Unbroken lines; various
combinations form interlacings 2,
3, 4, 5 and 6. 7. Two alternating
movements form the pattern.

GENERAL GUIDELINES

The realisation of ornament in all the applied arts is restricted by technical limitations, but technique is of special importance in Cluny lace. Indeed, it is impossible to design even the tiniest picot without taking into account the way in which it must be executed.

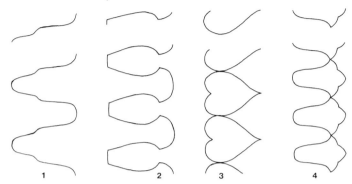

Figure 61
Unbroken lines arising from regular movements, based on natural or stylysed shapes.

As stated at the very beginning of this book, Cluny laces are essentially *interlacing lines,* which cross, join, and separate again. The main restriction of the technique is that these lines *cannot run upwards* (Fig. 60). Looking at the pattern as it will appear on the pillow, *the lines must always descend.*

As mentioned above, design of Cluny lace must begin with the study of unbroken lines with regular movements, which can be interlaced. Models for such movements are found not only in stylised ornament, but also in natural shapes. Placing such shapes next to each other will provide the basis for a design exercise (Fig. 61).

The various classic processes of composition, i.e. vertical or horizontal displacement of the chosen pattern, repetition and inversion, can also be used to create interlacing (Fig. 62). A pattern may be formed by following two different movements alternately (Fig. 62:7). The combination of two or three different movements can provide sufficient interest for even the

Figure 63
Interlacing of three linear
movements.

largest patterns (Figs. 63, 63b and Plates 9 – 9a). Once
the basic pattern of interlacing has been established it
must be decorated to transform it into a full lace
design.

Types of decoration include: the decoration of lines,
the decoration of crossings, and the creation of solid
areas.

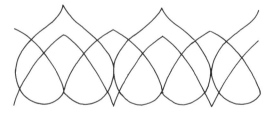

Figure 63b
Ornamental development of Figure
63.

The decoration of lines

Lines of the initial design may be doubled, widened by
means of clothwork, or replaced entirely by *decorated
lines* (see the preceding chapter). Any of these decora-
tions may follow a single line without interruption
(Fig. 64a), or it may switch from one line to another
(Fig. 64b).

35

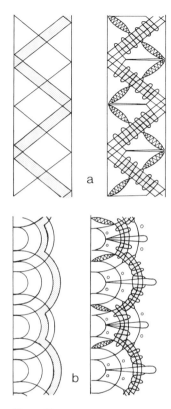

Figure 64
Ornamental development of a chosen theme: decoration of the lines.

The decoration of crossings

Crossings may be enlarged to form either solid or open areas or, alternatively, be transformed into motifs, as discussed in the section on decorated crossings, page 29. Naturally, the size of such motifs will depend on the number of pairs available. When there are not enough pairs their number may be increased, but the balance of the composition must not be disturbed.

The creation of solid areas

Solid areas are needed to avoid the monotony of too many linear elements together, and to create interesting *contrasts*.

It should be borne in mind that every solid area must have a certain number of lines leading to it, from the plaits which supply the necessary pairs. In Figure 65a the solid areas are *impossible* to make because there is nothing to make them with. The examples in Figure 65b show how a sufficient number of plaits converge and make the solid area possible. These solid areas can be regarded as decorated crossings and therefore as an extension of the preceding section. The care with which solid areas must be treated cannot be overemphasised; ideally *every pair* should be indicated by a line. At the very least the course of the weavers must be inked in, since every change of direction will require a pin in the pricking.

To prepare the final pricking it is necessary to examine the rough design critically in order to show clearly the position of every pin.

PRACTICAL CONSIDERATIONS

A *good* design should be quick to make. The number of bobbins required should therefore not be too large, always bearing in mind the width of the lace. There should not be too many complicated crossings or tallies; the pattern should never involve working upwards; and finally the design should not be too complex and require too much concentration. To the person buying the lace, it is important that it should withstand normal use, especially washing, and that its

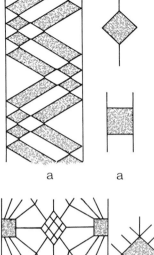

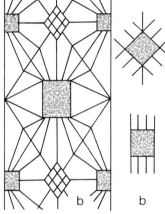

Figure 65
Solid areas. a. Areas impossible to make. b. Possible areas.

appearance is in keeping with the price.

The term 'practical considerations' sums up the above requirements. They must always be kept in mind.

Another requirement which must be observed is that the work should be strong an stable. To achieve this, construction lines are *essential*. In addition to the footside the following construction lines may also be needed: one or more lines parallel with the footside to prevent stretching lengthwise; lines across the pattern to prevent distortions in width. Additional straight lines in either direction will support curves and keep corners in shape. These construction lines must always be incorporated in such a way that they contribute to the appearance of the lace.

To summarise, the design of Cluny lace includes (Fig. 66 and Plate 10): a. The development of a basic pattern or combination of interlacing patterns. b. The incorporation of construction lines, which ensure stability of the lace in all directions. c. Decoration of the chosen theme.

It is necessary always to bear in mind the technical possibilities and the practical restrictions discussed above. The aim must be "to think constantly in terms of the actual working (of the lace)" (Edme Couty).

THE PRICKINGS

Earlier on we saw that prickings must be made from strong cardboard. Generally, they show only the pinholes, without any indication of the actual lace design. This kind of pricking needlessly complicates the task of the lacemaker, who cannot check whether the pricking is correct, or see clearly what she is supposed to do. The work of the lacemaker will be much easier, *and* give better results if the design is reproduced on the pricking★.

★Originally the lacemaker often used a sample as a working model in addition to the plain pricking. These were prepared by a special group of experienced workers *(echantillonneuses)*. The lacemaker could dispense with the sample by inking in the pattern in sufficient detail on her pricking.

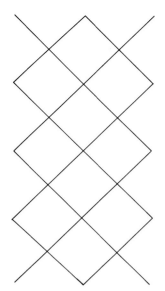
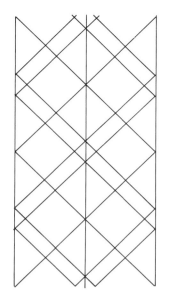
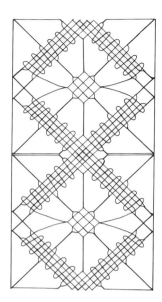

Figure 66
Three stages in the design of a piece
of Cluny lace.

The length of a pricking depends to some extent on the size of the individual motifs, but it is usually about 25 to 30 cm (10 – 12 in) long. The first and last 3 to 4 cm (1.5 in) of the pricking must be identical, and must be prepared with extra care. The reason is that when the lacemaker reaches the bottom of the pricking, she must be able to move the work up to the top again. To do this she must remove all the pins and after moving the lace to the top of the pricking, replace a sufficient number of pins *in the corresponding pinholes,* to keep the lace from being pulled out of shape★.

★With modern pillows, which contain a roller or removable blocks, it is better to have *two* identical prickings which are used alternately. It is then no longer necessary to remove *all* the pins at any stage; this saves a great deal of time and trouble. Note that it will still be necessary to have top and bottom of both prickings exactly the same, in order to overlap them when the work proceeds from the bottom of one pricking to the top of the other.

PART FOUR
Working Medallions or Insertions

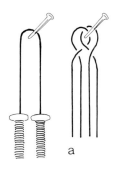

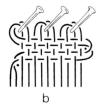

Figure 67
Starting a plait or a clothwork area.

Figure 68
Single and double loop used to keep the thread from unwinding.

MATERIALS AND INSTRUCTIONS

To make round, square, triangular or irregular medallions in Cluny lace a *movable pillow* is essential, to allow the orientation of the work to be changed. With such a pillow relatively short pins are used which are pushed right in, while on a fixed pillow the pins can be long, and are pushed in only half way. The hook or needle pin, which is never used for *straight* Cluny lace, is essential here. The needle pin is made from a medium size sewing needle with a slightly curved point, fixed to a small wooden handle. A fine crochet hook may also be used.

Setting up and finishing off will require greater care than with straight lace: pairs should be introduced and removed invisibly, making as few knots as possible.

To set up the border of a medallion

Several threads will be needed, each with a bobbin at either end (1).

Every thread is hung over a pin in such a way, that there is one bobbin on each side of the pin, at the same distance from it. Two threads will require four bobbins (Fig. 67a).

The lacemaker starts with the band which usually borders the medallion, by hanging the bobbins from a row of pins in the manner just described. Although this band will involve curves or corners, the work must always remain very regular.

A corner is worked according to one of the two diagrams in Figure 69. In *a* the clothwork has three pairs of passives, and shows a row of twisted cloth stitches on the outer edge only. In *b* the clothwork has also three pairs of passives, but now both edges have

---

1. To prepare these: knot the threads of two bobbins together. Unwind about 60 cm (24 in) of thread from one bobbin, and wind it onto the other bobbin. Secure each bobbin with a loop (Fig. 68), to prevent the threads from unwinding. When the knot is reached in the course of the work, carry the section of thread with the knot in it around a convenient pin, put the bobbin back in place and continue with the work. When the lace is finished, cut away the loop which has been formed in this way. The thread will be kept safely in place by the rest of the work.

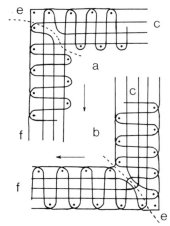

Figure 69
Making corners in a cloth stitch
band: After the area between *c* and
the dotted line has been worked,
the pillow is given a quarter-turn.
b shows the orientation of the
pattern while working the section
up to the corner. After turning the
pillow, section *e–f* will face the
worker.

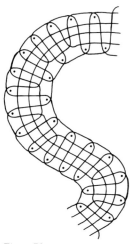

Figure 70
Making curves in a cloth stitch
band. Note the exchange of
weavers on the inside of the curves.

a row of twisted cloth stitches. Every time the band
changes direction, i.e. when the work has reached
point *e,* the pillow must be given a quarter turn, to
keep the bobbins pointing towards the worker.

Corners and curves in the border

When the band describes a wide curve, the technique
remains the same, only the pins on the inside of the
curve are placed a little closer together than on the outside. When the curve is very sharp, it will be necessary
to exchange the weavers on the inside of the clothwork, so that the threads are not too crowded
(Fig. 70).

Sewing out the threads of the border

When the band has been worked round the entire
medallion, it reaches the starting point where it must
be joined and the threads cut. This join is made as
follows (Fig. 71):

> Take out pin No. 1; insert the hook into the small
> loop and pull through the thread from the first

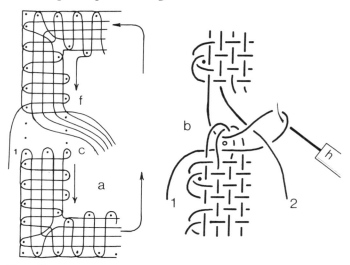

Figure 71
Finishing off the cloth stitch band:
The free end *f* must be attached to
the beginning *c.* b. shows a sewing
in detail.

bobbin. The first thread now forms a loop, and the second bobbin is passed through this loop. Both threads must be drawn up carefully, then tied with a double knot. They may now safely be cut. Then a second pair from the band is sewn into the same loop. The other pairs are sewn into the remaining small loops in the same manner, and the pins are taken out as the work progresses. Each pair must be knotted before being cut.

Introducing pairs for the centre of the medallion

After the border has been completed, the pairs which will form the centre of the medallion must be attached to it. This is also done by means of sewings.

Suppose that one pair is to be attached (Fig. 72): take a thread about 20 cm (8 in) long, with a bobbin at each end, and take out the pin supporting the small loop. Insert the hook; pick up the thread with the hook halfway between the bobbins and pull it through, forming a large loop. Pass one of the bobbins through the loop to form a slip-knot. Tighten the sewing by pulling both ends of the thread.

When two pairs are to be attached to the same loop, as in Figure 73: 4e, two threads must be prepared, each with a bobbin at either end. After a loop from one of the threads has been pulled through as before, a bobbin attached to the *second* thread is passed through it. The sewing is tightened, and a simple knot is made with two of the threads, as in Figure 72b.

Finally, when a greater number of pairs is to be attached to the same loop, the above procedure is simply repeated (Fig. 73: 8e).

Not all pairs needed for the centre of the medallion start at the border. For instance, the pairs which will form the square *CDFG* in Figure 73 start in a corner, at *C*. (See also the top diagram in Figure 73H).

After making a plait from *8e4s* to *C*, put up a temporary pin in *O,* and on this pin hang two new pairs. Make a windmill crossing supported by a pin at *C*. Now take out the temporary pin at

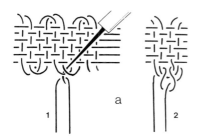

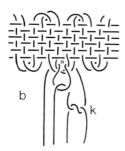

Figure 72
Adding 1 or 2 pairs by means of sewings.

41

O, and pull up the new threads. They are now ready to make the plait as indicated in the drawing. When the square has been completed, the threads must be sewn, knotted and cut at the same point, C.

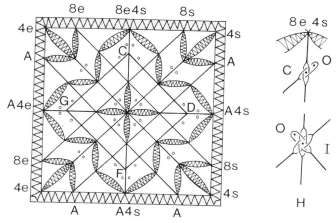

Figure 73
Example of square medallion.
A: Adding pairs; *4e, 8e:* 2 or 4 pairs enter the centre of the medallion. *4s, 8s:* 2 or 4 pairs are sewn out. *H:* Details showing how to add 2 new pairs to a plait or to a crossing of two plaits.

When two new pairs must be introduced at a point where two plaits cross each other (see lower diagram of Figure 73H), hang the new pairs on a temporary pin at O, and work an ordinary 3-plait crossing, supported by a pin at I. When the crossing is completed take out the temporary pin and pull up the new threads, which are then ready to make the plait (1).

A sewing must be made when a bar or a plait meets the border surrounding the medallion (Fig. 73); the same applies whenever a part being worked is to join a part already completed. The thread nearest the completed part is used to make the loop, and the next bobbin is passed through it. In the case of a 2-pair plait, one can either make a sewing with just two threads, or make a double sewing. In the latter case two threads are pulled through to form a loop, and the two remaining bobbins are passed through it.

1. These technical details, and also those of Figure 76, have been given by Miss van Houtte.

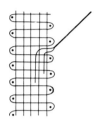

Figure 74
Incorporating pairs in the
clothwork.

Figure 75
Example of a circular medallion.
Two pairs enter at *e,* and two pairs
are sewn out at *s. D:* Pairs are
temporarily incorporated in the
clothwork. *A:* The pairs leave the
clothwork again.

Once the work is completed, threads are taken out
by sewings and knots, as for the border of the
medallion.

When a section is to be joined to a clothwork area
being worked, knots may be avoided by incorporating
the threads for a short distance in the clothwork. These
threads are then simply cut off close to the clothwork
(Fig. 74). This procedure should be adopted wherever
the design allows it. Similarly the cutting of the
threads which enter the clothwork and emerge at a
point close by can be avoided by including them in the
clothwork for a short distance. Figure 75 is an example
of this. Threads enter at *e,* and are sewn out at *s*; at *D* 4
threads enter the border clothwork, and at *A* they
leave again. Obviously, in this case the border is
worked at the same time as the rest of the medallion.

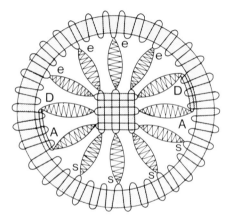

Working border and centre simultaneously
Although working the border of the medallion first
requires the least amount of thought by the lacemaker,
it is sometimes advantageous to work the border and
the centre simultaneously. Often many knots and
sewings may be avoided in this way. Figure 76, which
shows the beginning of a circular motif, is an example.

At *A* put in a row of pins and hang two pairs over
each pin. The top two will form two weaver
pairs. These workers make twisted cloth stitch

through two sets of passive pairs: one set of four passive pairs to the left, and another set of four to the right. First, work with the weavers to the right, pass round pin *1*, come back to the inside of the border, and lay them aside. Hang two more pairs on pin *2* and on pin *3* as before, according to Figure 76. Three of the four new pairs will be used for the clothwork section *T*.

At *E*, two 2-pair plaits must be introduced. Diagram *b* shows how to do this: after pin *5* take the workers to the inside of the curve, and lay them aside. Hang two new pairs from pin *7*; work one of these to the inside of the curve, and lay it next to pin *6*, on which two more pairs should be hung. At pin *6* there are now four pairs of bobbins: two to the right and two to the left of the pin. Twist pairs *2* and *4* over pairs *1* and *3*; then cross pair *2* over pair *3*. The bobbins are now ready to work the two plaits starting from pin *6*.

Figure 76b shows at *F* how four new plaits are introduced at one point instead of two (each thin line in

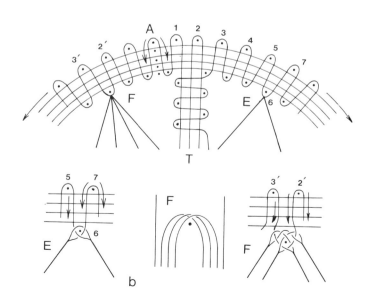

44

the figure represents one pair of threads, as usual). Here *six* new pairs are hung on pin *6* instead of two. On each side of the pin there will now be four pairs: three new pairs, and one pair coming from pin 2′ or pin 3′ of the border. (Fig. 76F).

> [Counting from the left and picking up two bobbins at a time: cross pair 4 over pair 5 *twice*– take out the pin and put it back in the centre of all the pairs – move the extreme right-hand pair to the left three times, by going over, under and over the next pair to the left – weave the extreme left-hand pair to the right four times, by going under, over, under and over the next pair to the right. The bobbins are now ready to make the four plaits.]

Medallions may be made in a great number of different shapes, and it is impossible to foresee every single problem which may be encountered. However, such problems will normally be similar to those already encountered: adding and removing pairs; pairs which are included temporarily in a cloth stitch area, only to emerge a little later on; sewings, etc . . .

It must be left to the initiative of the lacemaker to find the best way to work each pattern accurately, firmly and beautifully.

POINTS TO REMEMBER

Limitations of technique are less restricting for medallions than for straight lace. Although this allows greater freedom, this is nevertheless limited by the following requirements: The pairs must, if possible, be added or removed at edges; when new pairs must be added in the middle of the medallion, they should be used as fully as possible to justify the extra trouble involved.

As a general rule, the lace designer must see that knots are made where they will be least obvious, i.e. close to cloth stitch areas and not in the middle of an arrangement of plaits where they will be very conspicuous.

Finally, straight lines across the medallion, in several directions, are *essential* to keep all the elements firmly in place (Pls. 11, 12).

As for ideas for the design of medallions, it seems natural to look for them in geometrical combinations, as they offer countless possibilities which are very well suited to the neat and logical character of Cluny lace. Of course, freer and less regular shapes drawn from nature may also be explored, but these can be much more easily and better expressed in other types of lace, such as guipures, Flemish and Bruges lace.

Only by aiming at a prefect balance between the decorative idea and the constraints imposed by technique can one seek perfection and avoid the degeneration of any type of lace.

PART FIVE
New Material

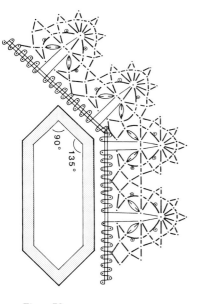

Figure 78
Example of a corner which does not form a right angle.

Figure 79
Design specially adapted for a scarf-end.

CORNERS

Lace used to be bought either by the yard or as a finished piece. The former had to be mitred or simply gathered to form corners. In the larger pieces, such as wedding handkerchiefs or collars, corners formed an integral part of the whole design. Lace is now no longer made by hand commercially but the practice lives on as a very satisfying hobby, which allows much more time to be spent on the appearance and finishing of every piece. Making a corner to match a straight lace design is well worth the extra effort.

Many of the existing designs for straight Cluny lace can be adapted to create corners. The basic design element of simple linear movement lends itself readily to the (usually slight) rearrangement which will be necessary.

Most corners will need to be right angles, but don't forget that other angles are also worth considering (Fig. 78). A curved shape could be attractive around the neckline of a dress, or on a round cloth. If the lace is to be applied entirely onto material instead of being added to the edge, it becomes possible to have the foot-side on the *outside* of the corner, as shown in the second corner for Pattern 6, Plate 6a. A specially adapted corner design may be convenient if you want to add lace to the end of a scarf or to the two ends of a table runner (Fig. 79). This brings the threads round so that the ends can be concealed in a side seam. When making a completely new design rather than adapting existing lace, keep the idea of a corner in mind from the outset. This will lead to better integration of the corner and the straight lace.

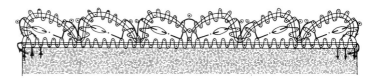

The one essential accessory for creating a corner is a small hand-mirror, with the reflecting surface extending right up to the edge. This mirror is moved along

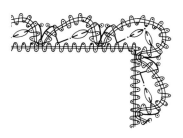

Figure 80
An asymmetrical corner.

the length of the straight design, or better still along the lace itself, at the desired angle, which is 45 degrees for a 90 degree corner. You will find that there are usually several places where a possible corner (half real and half reflected in the mirror) suggests itself.

If the mirror alone does not spark off any ideas, try making a few copies of the design, and cut them up into parts which form more or less self-contained units. Then just play around with these, to see if you can find an arrangement which might be suitable. This last approach is particularly useful when the original design is not symmetrical (Fig. 80).

For any of the possible solutions you must then check if the corner can actually be made, and also if the design of the corner will blend successfully with that of the original lace.

The corner should be a natural extension of the straight lace. If this has, for instance, prominent flowing lines, these should not be interrupted, but instead be carried smoothly from one straight side to the other. If the straight lace has marked scallops, a corner is usually possible at the narrowest point *between* two repeats. This arrangement should be avoided however, because it makes the corner look very skimpy compared with the rest of the lace (Fig. 81). Draw a line along the headside, parallel to the footside. At the corner the lace should not fall away from this line too soon, but fill the whole of the corner area as fully as possible.

As far as the working is concerned, the corner should not introduce new problems, apart from perhaps a sewing or two. In particular the need for extra pairs should be carefully considered. These pairs may be spotted as follows: If you have your mirror in position, imagine that you are working the real part, up to the mirror. There all pairs should eventually cross over into the reflected part. If at any point you seem to need a pair which must come out of the mirror as it were, or which lies just on the 'break' line, you will in reality need to add a new pair, and *to remove it as well!* The only case where this would be accept-

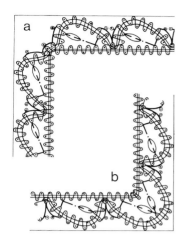

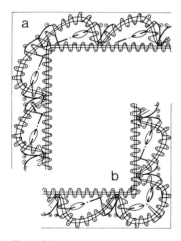

Figure 81
Examples of corner designs. In both cases *b* is a better solution than *a*.

able in practice is when the new pair(s) can be finished off invisibly and firmly. This means that they must be incorporated into an area of cloth stitch, and after at least 1 cm (0.5 in) removed unobtrusively. Unfortunately Cluny lace is essentially an open, plaited lace, and clothwork areas are used only sparingly. As a rule the addition of new pairs for a corner should therefore be avoided. Consider also the following: after the lace has been laundered, the corners will probably be pulled into shape more thoroughly than other parts of the lace. Any threads and knots not firmly secured will eventually be pulled apart. If you intend your lace to be *used*, why weaken it in the very places which require the greatest strength.

When you have decided where and how you are going to make the corner, you can start making the pricking for it. For each half of the corner make a copy of the straight design for as far as you are going to use it. This will probably include three or more repeats on one half, and at least one repeat on the other. You can cut up photocopies, or else make your two halves by hand on tracing paper. (Transparent graph paper can be even more useful than plain tracing paper.) Assemble the two halves and then decide on the place for any extra pinholes that may be needed, and perhaps change the place of a few of the original pinholes as well.

You now have your master copy of the new corner. Do not be tempted to use this to make the actual pricking on cardboard. Once you have pricked through it, it will no longer photocopy satisfactorily, and you would have to make up a new master copy if you ever wanted to share your work with a friend. If is far better to make a fresh copy of your master, and use this instead to prick through. Do not forget to ink in as much of the design on the pricking as is necessary, to allow you to work it without reference to the original.

Working Notes on the Prickings

Pattern 1, Plates 1 and 1a

10 pairs, linen No. 60.

Start with 4 pairs at the footside. Make a windmill crossing on the first pin, as shown in Figure 82. Add the other pairs, two at a time, at the points indicated on the pricking; see also Figure 83. Where 2 plaits meet at the footside do not make a windmill crossing, but make either a join (Fig. 84a) or a fast crossing (p. 9) with both pairs of the footside-plait and one pair of the other plait (Fig. 85a). In the corner the plait forming the footside makes a simple join with the plait next to it (Fig. 84b).

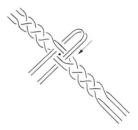

Figure 82
Starting two 2-pair plaits from one pin.

Figure 83
Adding two pairs, starting from a plait.

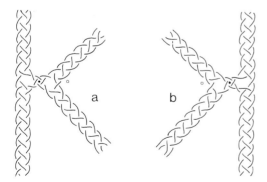

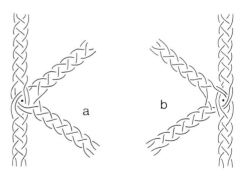

Figure 84
Joining two plaits at the footside or at the headside.

Figure 85
Joining two plaits with a *fast crossing*.

Plate 1a

Plate 1

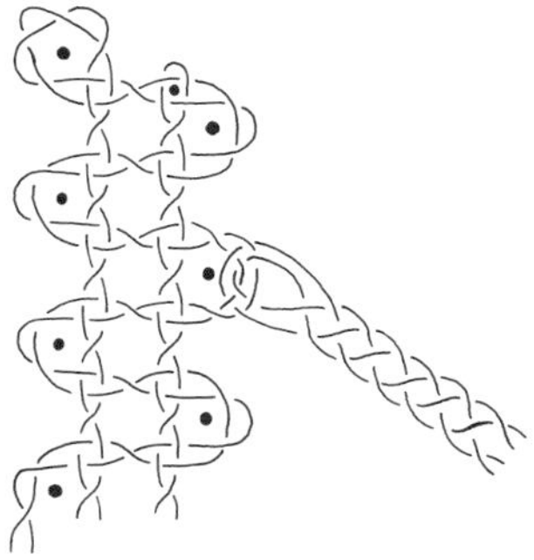

Figure 86
Starting a plait from the footside.

Pattern 2, Plates 2 and 2a

11 pairs, linen No. 60.

Add the pairs according to the numbers indicated on the pricking. Start with the footside (Fig. 86). After the pairs for the first plait have been added, leave them until the footside has been worked as far as possible; then work the plait, pulling the pairs as little as possible. The remaining 6 pairs are started separately (Fig. 82 and 83). Where the weaver pair leaves the footside it forms a 1-pair bar which needs special attention. It meets a plait five times before returning to the footside. The first, third and fifth time only one pair of the plait is used for the connection, which is made as shown in Figure 25; the second and fourth time the bar crosses straight through the plait. Note that the 2 pairs which trace the line with the leaves, and the weaver pair of the footside do not interchange with the other pairs, only with each other. Therefore these 3 pairs offer a good opportunity to introduce coloured threads.

Plate 2

Plate 2a

Pattern 3, Plates 3 and 3a

12 pairs, linen No. 60.
Start with 4 pairs at each of the three pinholes at the
top of the pricking (Fig. 82). The connections with the
footside and the headside plaits are made as fast
crossings, see Figure 85a–b and page 9. For the 4-
pair plait in the centre, see Figures 7 and 8.

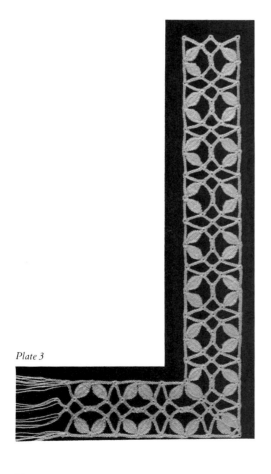

Plate 3

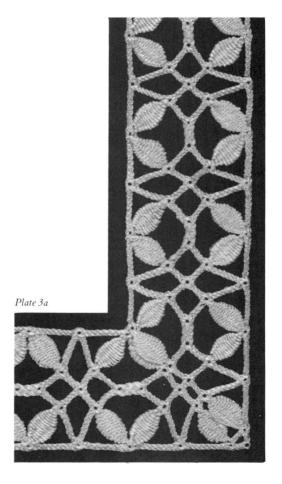

Plate 3a

Figure 87
Starting 6 new pairs at the top of a circle.

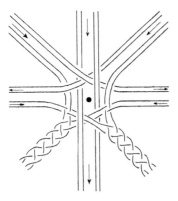

Figure 88
Centre of the circle for Pattern 4.

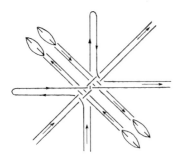

Figure 89
Centre of the corner circle for Pattern 4.

Pattern 4, Plates 4 and 4a

14 pairs, linen No. 60.

Start with 4 pairs at each of the top two pinholes (Fig. 82); the remaining 6 pairs start from the top of the circle, as illustrated in Figure 87. The 6-pair plaits connecting the circles are made similarly to ordinary plaits, but picking up 3 bobbins instead of 1 for each movement. To start the 6-pair plait: after the 3-plait crossing (Fig. 21b) which closes the circle, divide the 4 bobbins of the centre plait over the 4 pairs of the other two plaits, so that four groups of 3 bobbins are formed. To finish the 6-pair plait: work almost up to the start of the next circle, and then take from each of the 4 groups of 3 bobbins 1 bobbin; lay these 4 bobbins side by side to form the new centre plait; now proceed to make the 3-plait crossing (Fig. 21b) which starts the circle.

In the centre of the circle there are two possible ways to form the horizontal 1-pair bars: a. Two 1-pair bars leave the centre of the circle, and after connecting to the edges, return to the centre. This could be done according to Figures 88 (centre) and 84 (edges). b. A 1-pair bar leaves the footside, goes all the way to the headside, and returns to the footside. The crossing in the centre is similar to that in Figure 23a. In the corner the 1-pair bar *must* be worked similarly to *a* above, see also Figure 89 for a possible solution.

55

Plate 4a

Plate 4

56

Pattern 5, Plates 5, 5a and 5b

29 pairs, linen No. 110.

Although this lace looks complicated, it is not very difficult to make. Note that in each scallop four sewings will be needed: two in the centre and two more where a plait runs unexpectedly in the opposite direction of the twisted cloth stitch band (see the small arrows in the pricking). To facilitate sewing into a plait, you could loop a doubled thread through the plait while it is being made (Fig. 90). The large amount of passive pairs at the footside between two scallops makes it impossible to finish them all off invisibly. One solution could be simply to extend the cloth stitch area at the footside a little and then make a plain seam, pressed open as in ordinary sewing! The 6 remaining pairs must be sewn out separately as invisibly as possible.

Figure 90
A doubled thread will make sewing into a plait easier.

Plate 5b

Plate 5a

Plate 5

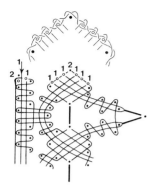

Figure 91
Setting up Pattern 6.

Pattern 6, Plates 6, 6a, 6b and 6c

12 pairs, linen No. 60.

The pricking gives two different corners. Use as many repeats of the straight part as needed, and follow Figure 91 when setting up the lace. Sewings will be necessary in the corners. The two little cross–lines in one of the corners also indicate sewings; in this case a 1–pair bar is sewn twice to another bar, to simulate a plait.

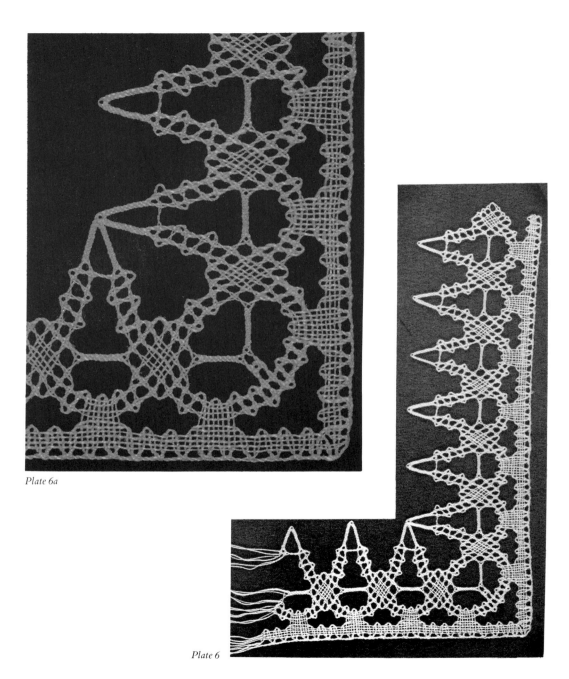

Plate 6a

Plate 6

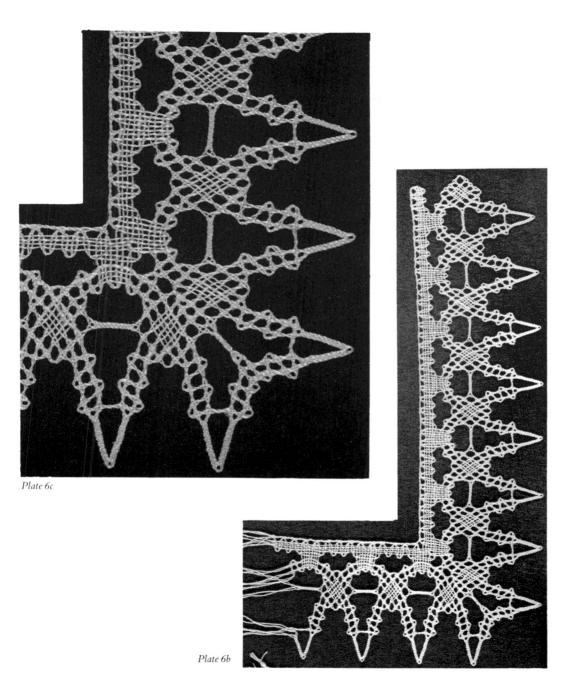

Plate 6c

Plate 6b

63

Figure 93
A double knotted picot.

Pattern 7, Plates 7 and 7a

26 pairs, linen No. 60.

The square areas are nothing but very elaborate crossings, made in one of the many variations of the so-
called Rose Ground. Although Cluny lace does not
have a background net, ground stitches such as these
can work very well in small areas. In the corner simply
work up to the diagonal, and then turn your pillow as if
you were making Torchon lace. Rose ground is well
suited to this kind of treatment, but if you look closely,
you will see that the two halves of the corner square
have been worked in different directions. Figure 92
shows the course of the threads for the *corner* square.

The tallies are *not* leaves, since they are not pointed
where they meet the squares. When working the Rose
Ground you must therefore be very careful when you
pull up a thread which has served as a weaver for a
tally.

The double picots can be made as shown in Figure
93. Both picots are made with the same thread; this
prevents weakening of the plait, but also stops the
picots being exactly opposite each other. If your lace
will not be washed, you could make the picots symmetrical by using a different thread for each. In that
case see Figure 29.

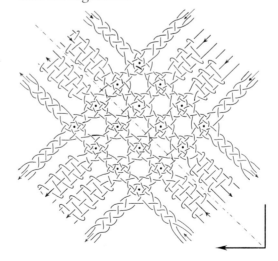

Figure 92
Detail of the corner for Pattern 7.

64

Plate 7a

Plate 7

65

Pattern 8, plates 8 and 8a

18 pairs, linen No. 60.

This insertion presents no new difficulty. Note that the connections to the plaits at the edges are worked according to Figure 84, but with the pin placed as indicated by the small open circle. Note the difference this makes to the appearance of the join!

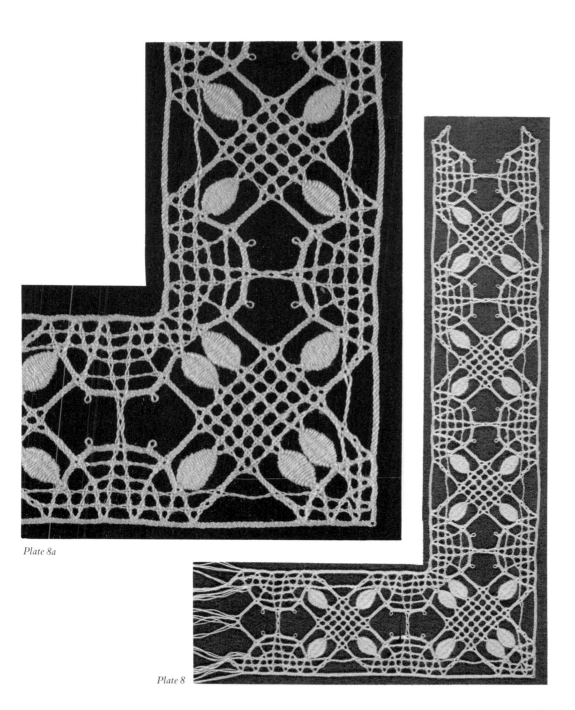

Plate 8a

Plate 8

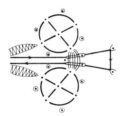

Figure 94
Dense area between two circles in
Pattern 9.

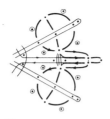

Figure 95
Dense area between two circles at
the edge of Pattern 9.

Pattern 9, Plates 9 and 9a

25 pairs, linen No. 60.

Most of this lace is straight-forward to make; you will
find it saves time if you first work as far as you can on
one side of the twisted cloth stitch trail, then work one
whole section of twisted cloth stitch, and then work as
far as possible on the other side. For the dense areas
between two circles, see Figures 94 and 95. In both
Figures the circle is closed with a 3-plait crossing using
Method II (Fig. 21b), and the pairs of each plait make
one more whole stitch. Then, as in Figure 94 work in
cloth stitch with each of the two pairs from the plait
through the 6 pairs of the circle. The plait is then connected twice with the cloth stitch trail before being
worked back in the same way. In Figure 95 the 1-pair
bar coming from the main trail is worked in cloth
stitch through the first 4 pairs out of the 6 from the
circle. The remaining 2 pairs form one of the two plaits
used in the point. The other plait is formed from the
1-pair bar and the last (i.e. the 4th) pair it worked
through. On the way back one pair of this plait again
becomes a 1-pair bar, the other is left behind to form
part of the centre plait for the new circle. Before making the 3-plait crossing which begins the second circle,
start each of the 3 plaits with one cloth stitch.

The solid area where two leaves meet is made as
illustrated in Figure 96. The shaded area is worked
entirely in cloth stitch. The 2 pairs from the incoming
leaf will meet 3 pairs coming out of the trail. At this
point treat all 5 pairs as single threads, as shown in the
Figure.

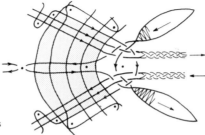

Figure 96
The solid area between two leaves
in Pattern 9.

Plate 9

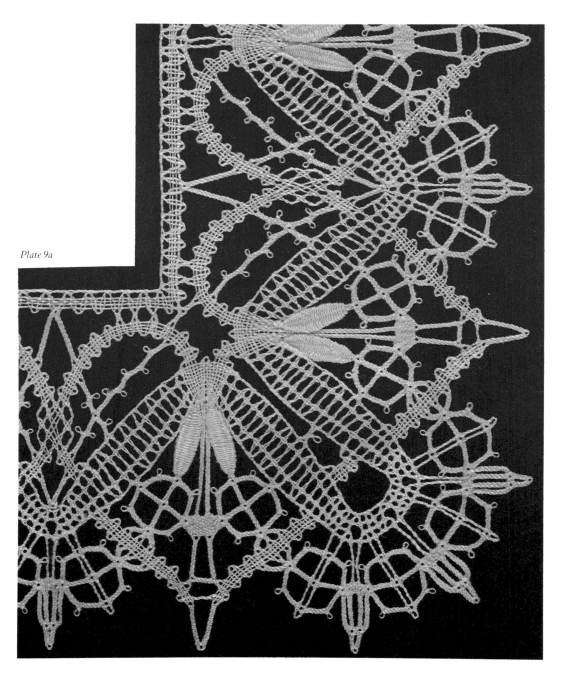

Plate 9a

Pattern 10, Plates 10 and 10a

20 pairs, linen No. 50.

In this lace you have the choice of starting the horizontal 1-pair bars either from the centre or from both edges. If you choose the latter, Figure 97 shows one way in which the 1-pair bar can leave and rejoin the edge.

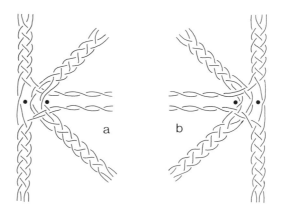

Figure 97
A possible way of joining the horizontal bars to the edges in Pattern 10.

Plate 10

Plate 10a

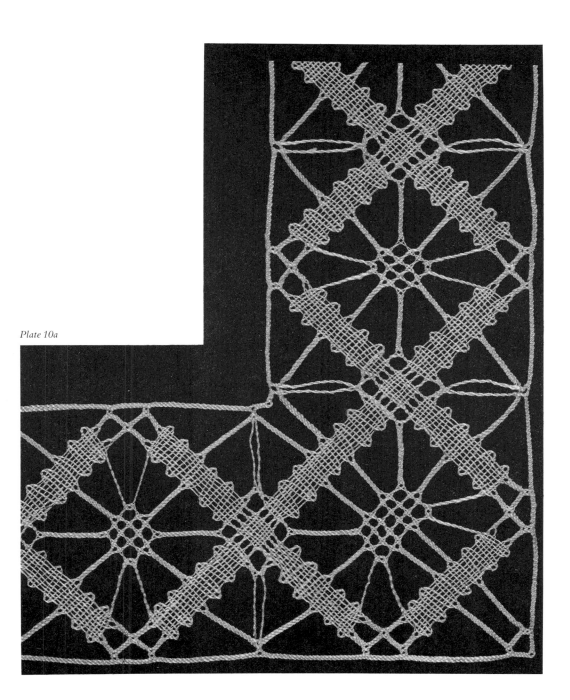

Pattern 11, Plates 11 and 11a

22 pairs linen No. 110.

Twelve out of the 22 pairs are started as a cloth stitch triangle, and if you study the pricking carefully you will see where the pairs are added. Four pairs are started just above the top of the first triangle: 2 for a plait, and 2 to form a passive and a weaver pair in the twisted cloth stitch trail. At the base of the next triangle another 4 pairs will be needed, and the remaining 2 pairs must be sewn in at the second corner to the twisted cloth stitch trail.

Plate 11

Pattern 12, Plates 12 and 12a

23 pairs linen No. 50.

This attractive medallion is by no means as simple to make as may seem. This is because the cloth stitch star in the centre needs to be worked as one unit. Therefore, at least 10 pairs will be needed to start it from two points, and even then it will be necessary to connect the 1-pair bars coming in from the edge by means of sewings. It is very important to start the circular cloth stitch trail (with 5 pairs) at the place indicated on the pricking. Study the arrows carefully in the course of the work. All the numbers on the pricking indicate where new pairs must be added. Note that 4 pairs must be started at the first point of the centre motif. When you are left with pairs which have nowhere else to go, you will have to sew them out.

Plate 12

Plate 11a

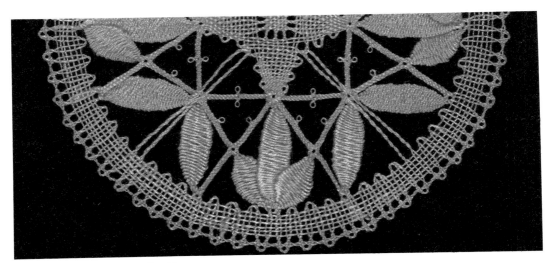

Plate 12a

Prickings

Pricking No 1

Pricking No 2

77

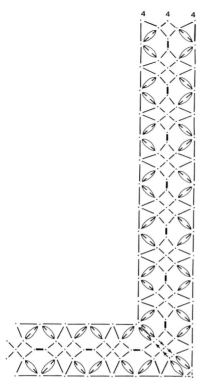

Pricking No 3

Pricking No 4

78

Pricking No 5

Pricking No 5a

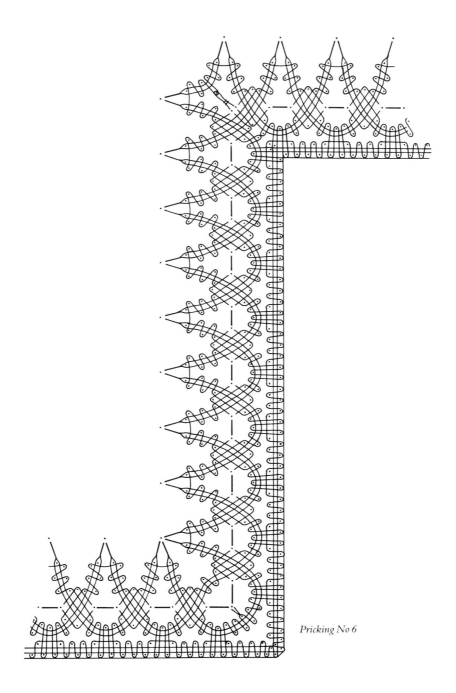

Pricking No 6

2 3 3 2

2 2

2 2 2 2

3 2

2 2

2 2

Pricking No 7

82

Pricking No 8

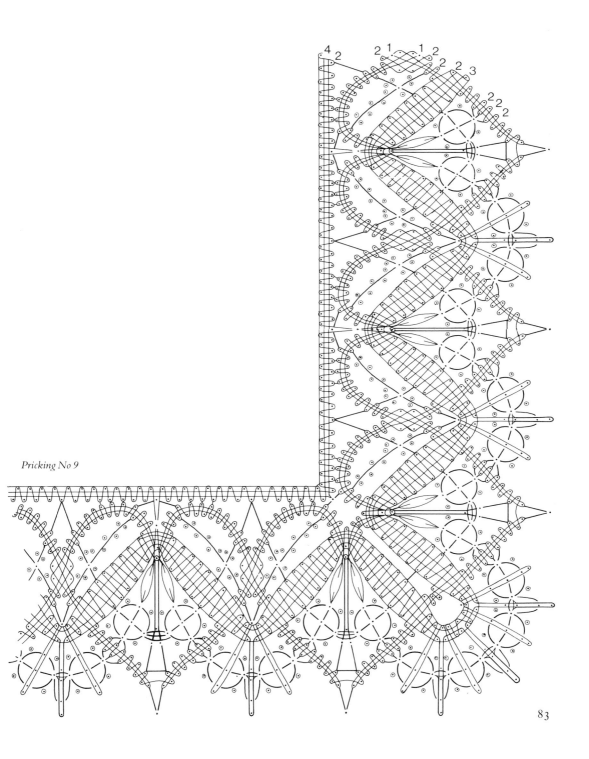

Pricking No 9

83

Pricking No 10

84

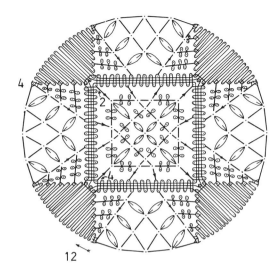

Pricking No 11

Pricking No 12